Polar
Worlds

A TEMPLAR BOOK
First published in the UK in 2009 by Templar Publishing,
An imprint of The Templar Company Limited,
The Granary, North Street,
Dorking,
Surrey,
RH4 1DN
www.templarco.co.uk

Conceived and produced by Weldon Owen Pty Ltd
59-61 Victoria Street, McMahons Point
Sydney, NSW 2060, Australia

WELDON OWEN GROUP
Chairman John Owen

WELDON OWEN PTY LTD
Chief Executive Officer Sheena Coupe
Creative Director Sue Burk
Concept Development John Bull, The Book Design Company
Art Manager Trucie Henderson
Senior Vice President, International Sales Stuart Laurence
Vice President, Sales: United States and Canada Amy Kaneko
Vice President, Sales: Asia and Latin America Dawn Low
Administration Manager, International Sales Kristine Ravn
Production Manager Todd Rechner
Production Coordinators Lisa Conway, Mike Crowton

Senior Editor Jasmine Parker
Designer Abi Cherokee
Illustrators Peter Bull Art Studio, Leonello Calvetti, Contact Jupiter (Rielle Levesque/
Polygone Studios, Yvan Meunier), Christer Eriksson

ISBN: 978-1-84011-741-7

Colour reproduction by Chroma Graphics (Overseas) Pte Ltd
Printed by SNP Leefung Printers Ltd
Manufactured in China

10 9 8 7 6 5 4 3 2 1

A WELDON OWEN PRODUCTION

insiders

Polar Worlds

Rosalyn Wade

templar publishing

Contents

introducing

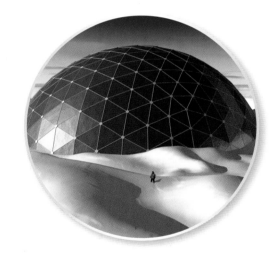

in *focus*

in*troducing*

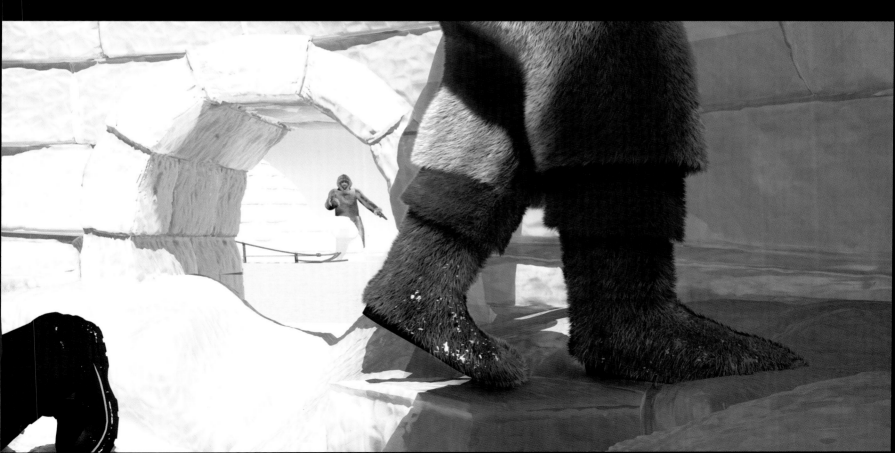

Into the Cold

The Poles

At the opposite ends of the world are the North and South Poles. They are surrounded by the polar regions. These icy wildernesses around the Poles are some of the most beautiful and dangerous landscapes on Earth. At the North Pole, at the top of the world, is a region called the Arctic, which is home to polar bears and snowy owls. At the other end of the world is the Antarctic continent, the area around the South Pole. Most of the world's penguins live in or near Antarctica. The polar regions are the coldest places on Earth. The lowest temperature ever recorded on Earth was in Antarctica— a chilling −89°C (−67°F).

South Pole *The South Pole is in Antarctica— the world's fifth largest continent. Most of Antarctica is covered by an ice sheet. The Antarctic ice sheet has a maximum depth of over 4.5 kilometres (2.8 mi) and is the largest ice sheet in the world.*

Opposite worlds

Polar winters are dark. On many days the Sun does not rise above the horizon. But in summer there are days when the Sun does not set. Some people call the polar regions the "land of the midnight Sun". These extreme seasons are caused by the tilt of Earth's axis leading the North and South Poles to take it in turn to face the Sun. The Arctic and Antarctic circles are imaginary lines that follow the limit of the midnight Sun and so mark the edges of the polar regions.

North Pole *The North Pole is located in the middle of the Arctic Ocean. The Arctic Ocean is Earth's shallowest ocean and is encircled by land.*

THE COLD POLES

In polar regions, the Sun's rays hit Earth's surface at a low angle. They have to travel further through Earth's atmosphere and warm a larger area than they would elsewhere.

Sun

North Pole

South Pole

Sea ice

Sea

Frozen sea *There is no land at the North Pole only sea ice, which covers much of the surface of the Arctic Ocean.*

South America

South Pacific Ocean

Arctic Ocean

Russia

Alaska

North Pole

Canada

Greenland

North America

Arctic Circle

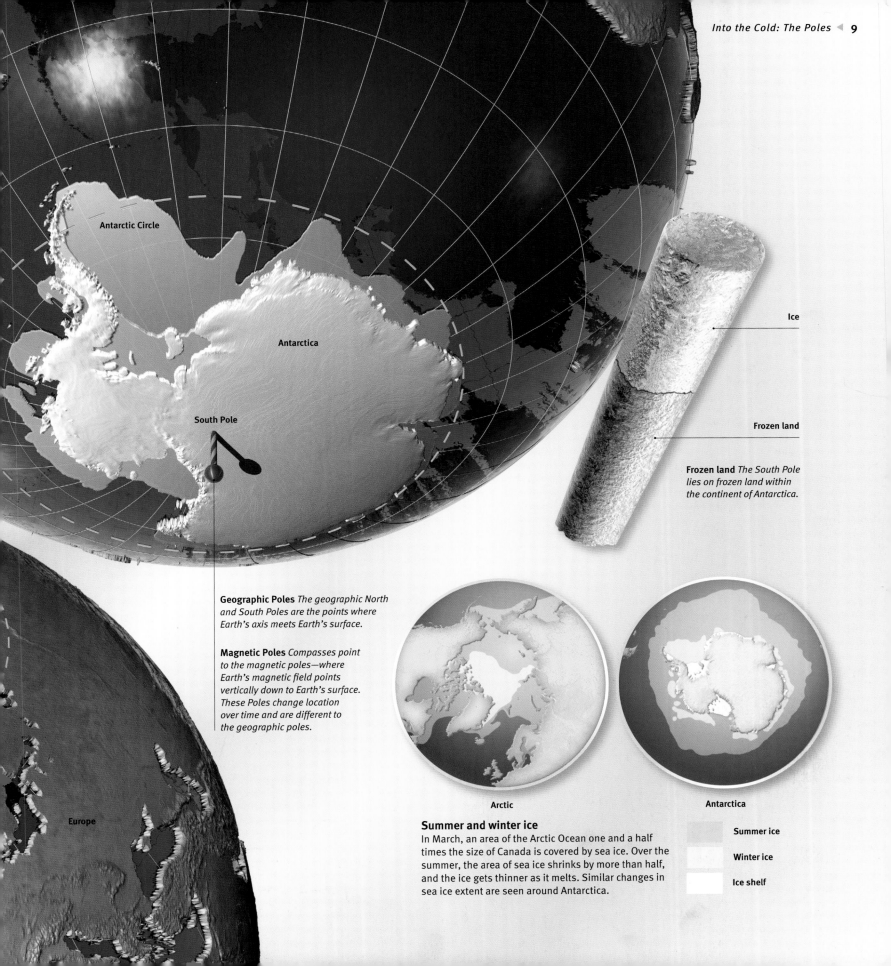

Antarctic Circle

Antarctica

South Pole

Ice

Frozen land

Frozen land *The South Pole lies on frozen land within the continent of Antarctica.*

Geographic Poles *The geographic North and South Poles are the points where Earth's axis meets Earth's surface.*

Magnetic Poles *Compasses point to the magnetic poles—where Earth's magnetic field points vertically down to Earth's surface. These Poles change location over time and are different to the geographic poles.*

Europe

Arctic

Antarctica

Summer and winter ice

In March, an area of the Arctic Ocean one and a half times the size of Canada is covered by sea ice. Over the summer, the area of sea ice shrinks by more than half, and the ice gets thinner as it melts. Similar changes in sea ice extent are seen around Antarctica.

Summer ice

Winter ice

Ice shelf

Polar
Environment

The temperature rarely rises above 0°C (32°F) in most of the Arctic and Antarctic. These frozen landscapes contain many different types of ice. On land, snow falls and gets packed down into glacial ice. Huge masses of glacial ice form the ice sheets that cover most of Antarctica and much of Greenland. These ice sheets are more than 2.5 kilometres (1.5 mi) thick and lock up most of the world's fresh water. In the extreme cold of the polar regions, the surface of the sea freezes to form sea ice. Sea ice spreads over much of the Arctic Ocean and around the coast of Antarctica. The amount of sea ice changes with the seasons. The Arctic and Antarctic are not entirely covered in snow and ice. In the summer, away from the poles, many areas are free of ice. A landscape populated with low-growing plants is uncovered in an ecosystem called tundra.

Aurora lights
Named after the Greek goddess of the dawn, auroras look like waves of red, green and blue light dancing in the night sky. The aurora australis or "southern lights" are seen in the Antarctic, and the aurora borealis or "northern lights" are seen in the Arctic.

Antarctic landscape

Antarctica is the coldest and windiest continent on Earth. It is classed as a desert because so little snow falls there. Over thousands of years enough ice has accumulated to form the largest ice sheet in the world. The Antarctic Ice Sheet covers 98 per cent of the continent and contains 70 per cent of the world's fresh water. There is little life on the continent, but many animals feast on the abundant krill in the cold, nutrient-rich waters around Antarctica.

Stripy iceberg
Icebergs come in many different shapes and sizes. This iceberg is a stripy or "striated" iceberg. The dark blue stripes are made of meltwater that has refrozen without any bubbles.

Falling snow

Fresh snowfall

Small granules of ice

Firn or compacting ice

Solid ice

Glacial ice formation
Much of the snow that falls in the Antarctic does not melt. As time goes by, layers of new snow bury the old, compacting it and turning it to ice.

Frozen sea ice *Salty sea water freezes just below 0°C (32°F) to form sea ice. The formation of sea ice passes through a number of stages.*

Types of sea ice:

1. **Frazil ice** *Frazil ice refers to small ice crystals that form in the surface water when it reaches freezing temperature.*

2. **Nilas** *If the ocean is calm, the frazil crystals come together to form a smooth sheet called nilas.*

3. **Pancake ice** *Rough water movement causes the ice crystals to form uneven plate shapes called pancake ice.*

4. **Pack ice** *Pack ice is solid and forms by wind and waves pushing together smaller pieces of ice.*

Ice sheet *The deeper layers of an ice sheet are under huge amounts of pressure, which causes the solid ice to flow downhill. Over time, this ice flows out onto the sea surface, where it forms a floating ice shelf.*

Glacier *A glacier is a large mass of compacted snow and ice that forms on land. The pull of gravity causes glaciers to travel downhill and towards the sea.*

Calving *Stresses cause icebergs to break off from ice sheets in a process called calving. Iceberg calving is responsible for around 90 per cent of the ice loss from the Antarctic Ice Sheet.*

Polar Ice

Iceberg

Icebergs are large pieces of ice that have broken off floating glaciers and ice shelves. Seawater erodes and weakens ice shelves and glaciers, which leads to iceberg calving. Sometimes an ice shelf breaks up simply because it is too large to support itself. Wind, waves and collisions may also cause icebergs to form. The ice of an iceberg is made of compacted snow and can be many thousands of years old. They range in size from a few metres long to hundreds of kilometres in length. Most of the ice lost from the Antarctic ice sheet is thought to be through iceberg calving. To date, the largest known icebergs have come from Antarctica's ice shelves.

Drifting mass

Once they have broken free of an ice shelf or glacier, icebergs are carried on ocean currents. Scientists have found drifting icebergs to be hotspots of biological activity, surrounded by more algae, krill and seabirds than nearby areas of iceberg-free ocean. Every iceberg is different. There are flat-topped icebergs, others are wedge shaped, and some blocky. Occasionally they roll over and expose their wave-eroded underside.

Visible top *Ice floats because it is less dense than water. The height of an iceberg above the sea's surface ranges from around 1 metre (3.3 ft) to 75 metres (246 ft).*

Hidden giant *Approximately 80–90 per cent of an iceberg lies beneath the surface of the water. The more dense an iceberg is, or the less air trapped inside it, the greater the amount of iceberg found underwater.*

Fin whales *These huge marine mammals are the second largest whales on Earth. They are filter feeders and sieve water for small marine animals. Fin whales are mostly found in oceans surrounding the Arctic and Antarctic.*

Shattering shelf

In early 2002, the Larsen B Ice Shelf on the Antarctic Peninsula collapsed. An area of 3,250 square kilometres (1,255 sq mi) of ice broke into small icebergs in just a few weeks.

31 January 2002

5 March 2002

TITANIC TRAGEDY

In April, 1912, the famous passenger steamship R.M.S. *Titanic* hit a large iceberg on its maiden voyage across the Atlantic Ocean. Just hours after the collision, the *Titanic* sank causing the death of 1,517 of its passengers and crew.

Polar Region
Plants

The polar regions are cold and dry. Less than one per cent of Antarctica is ice free and able to support plant life. Land plants are more abundant in the Arctic, even though the soil is often frozen. Plants are usually low-lying to avoid damage from strong winds. They also have a number of ways to avoid damage from extremely cold temperatures. The fluids of some polar plants freeze only at temperatures below -38°C (-36.4°F). Others allow ice to form in the fluid around their cells, keeping the cells themselves from freezing. All plants make the most of the short summer season to grow and reproduce.

Antarctic plants
The plants of subantarctic islands like South Georgia are low-growing, as in Arctic tundra areas. On Antarctica itself, conditions are too severe for many plants to grow. However, some lichens and mosses flourish here in the summer in sheltered areas.

Enticing glue *The leaves of the sundew are covered in bright red hairs. A gland at the end of each hair secretes a drop of glistening, sticky fluid that attracts insects.*

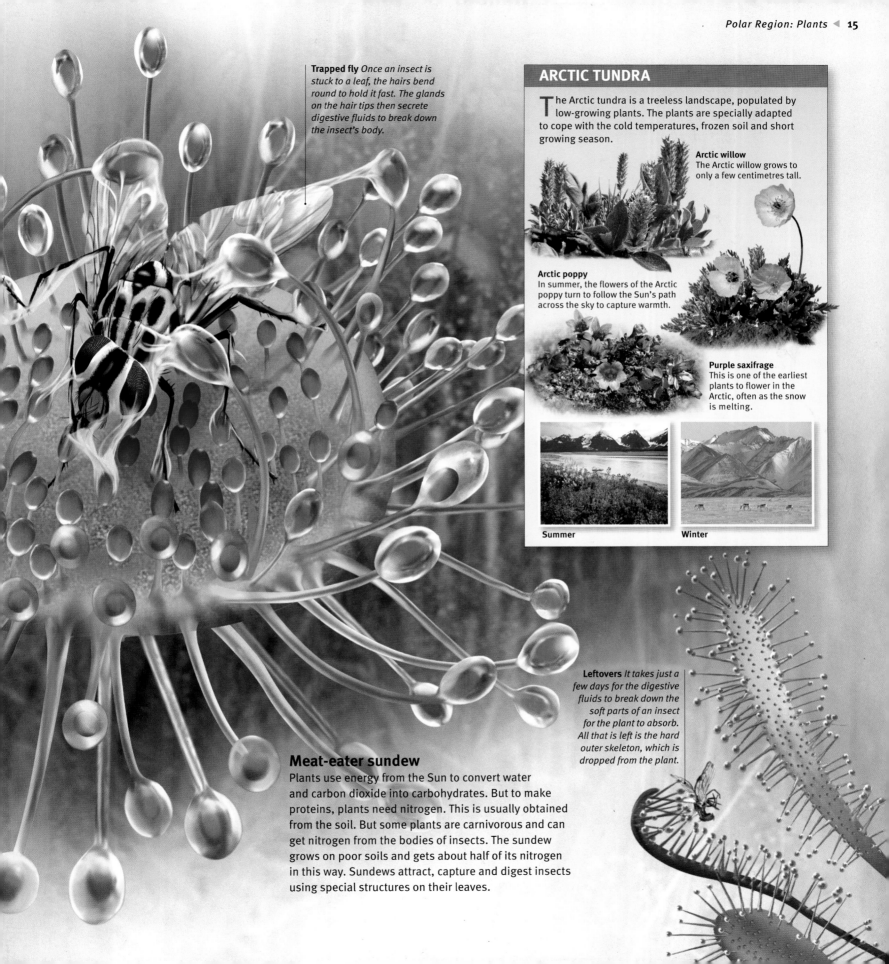

Trapped fly *Once an insect is stuck to a leaf, the hairs bend round to hold it fast. The glands on the hair tips then secrete digestive fluids to break down the insect's body.*

ARCTIC TUNDRA

The Arctic tundra is a treeless landscape, populated by low-growing plants. The plants are specially adapted to cope with the cold temperatures, frozen soil and short growing season.

Arctic willow
The Arctic willow grows to only a few centimetres tall.

Arctic poppy
In summer, the flowers of the Arctic poppy turn to follow the Sun's path across the sky to capture warmth.

Purple saxifrage
This is one of the earliest plants to flower in the Arctic, often as the snow is melting.

Summer

Winter

Leftovers *It takes just a few days for the digestive fluids to break down the soft parts of an insect for the plant to absorb. All that is left is the hard outer skeleton, which is dropped from the plant.*

Meat-eater sundew

Plants use energy from the Sun to convert water and carbon dioxide into carbohydrates. But to make proteins, plants need nitrogen. This is usually obtained from the soil. But some plants are carnivorous and can get nitrogen from the bodies of insects. The sundew grows on poor soils and gets about half of its nitrogen in this way. Sundews attract, capture and digest insects using special structures on their leaves.

Polar Survival
Animals

The Arctic is a dangerous place, with polar bears, wolf packs, glaucous gulls and snowy owls all on the attack. Large animals, such as walruses, are protected by their size. Others live in herds for safety in numbers. Some use speed to flee, or horns and tusks to defend themselves. Many smaller animals use camouflage to hide from predators. Arctic foxes change colour with the seasons. Their white coat blends into the snowy landscape of the Arctic winter; their brown coat merges with the snow-free tundra in summer. With this camouflage, Arctic foxes can hunt prey while hiding from predators.

High jumper *Arctic foxes leap high to land heavily and break the snow, then grab any small prey underneath. They also jump into the air to pin prey to the ground.*

Warmest fur *The Arctic fox's winter coat is twice as deep as its summer coat. The fur is the warmest of any animal, so these small predators can withstand temperatures of −70°C (−94°F).*

Winter white

In October, Arctic foxes develop their warmer winter coat of white, the same colour as the snow and ice. This camouflages them from polar bears and lets them creep up on prey such as lemmings. They also eat seabird eggs and berries, and scavenge on carcasses left by polar bears. When food is plentiful, foxes collect more than they need and bury it in the permafrost—frozen ground that never thaws and keeps the food fresh. They visit these caches in winter when food is scarce.

Summer coat

Arctic foxes shed their winter coat in April. A thinner, brown summer coat develops, which blends with the rocks and plants revealed when the snow melts. (Some foxes are dark blue-grey in summer and pale blue-grey in winter.) From April to July, females give birth to 6–12 cubs. The cubs leave the den after 2–4 weeks to explore and play-fight. The young foxes leave the family group by autumn to hunt alone.

Self-defence *Cubs learn to hunt and defend themselves while still with their parents. Play-fighting is important, but in years when food is scarce they spend more time resting and less time playing.*

COLOUR CHANGERS

Mammals' fur and birds' feathers change colour to blend in with the Arctic tundra's seasonal changes.

Arctic hare
They are white all year in the far north. Further south, they are brown in summer.

Willow ptarmigan
The brown feathers (males have a white underbelly) turn pure white in winter.

Arctic stoat
The brown coat with an off-white belly in summer changes to white winter fur.

Movement and
Life Cycles

The polar regions experience long hours of daylight in the summer. In winter, temperatures drop and the Sun does not rise above the horizon for weeks or even months. The seasons affect the amount of food that is available. In summer, polar waters are rich in food and plants are able to grow on land. Many polar animals time their breeding cycle for when food is plentiful. By the end of the short summer, young polar animals have to be strong enough to deal with either the harsh polar winter or the journey away from the Arctic or Antarctic. Many animals migrate away from the hostile polar environments before the onset of winter.

MACARONI DANCE

Macaroni penguins are monogamous—one male mates with one female. They reunite year after year at their nesting sites, recognising each other by their distinct calls. The "ecstatic dance", in which the penguins swing their heads from side-to-side, is an important part of their mating behaviour.

Long-distance travellers
Other polar animals also migrate to escape the harsh winters of the polar regions. The longest migration is made by the Arctic tern. It flies from the Arctic to the Antarctic and then back again.

Humpback whales
Some humpbacks migrate from their polar feeding waters in Antarctica to breed in Costa Rican waters—a distance of about 8,475 kilometres (5,265 mi).

Adélie penguin
Adélie penguins breed in Antarctica but migrate along the coastline to feeding grounds further north in the winter.

Barren ground caribou
These Canadian caribou, or reindeer, migrate north up to 1,290 kilometres (800 mi) to the coast and then return.

Feeding time
A female macaroni penguin lays two eggs in early November. Usually only the second egg survives and hatches after around 35 days. For the first three weeks, the male parent guards the chick, while the female collects food. Chicks then gather into creches, where the parents continue to feed them. About 60–70 days after hatching, the chicks grow waterproof feathers and can go to sea to forage for themselves.

Crop *Penguins often collect more food than they can hold in their beaks. A pouch in their food pipe, called a "crop", allows them to store food to regurgitate later.*

Orange plume *Macaroni penguins were named after the Macaroni hat. Their plume of orange feathers looked like the feathers on the hat.*

Savoury sludge *Macaroni penguins eat mainly krill, but also eat fish and squid. The adult eats the food and regurgitates it later for their chick.*

Hungry chick *Less than three weeks old, this chick is still being fed at the nest every day. It reaches into the throat of the adult penguin to receive regurgitated food.*

Nesting ground *Macaroni penguins nest on rocky slopes or beaches on islands north of Antarctica.*

Racing North
Arctic Explorers

For centuries, men have set out on expeditions to the Arctic Ocean. William Edward Parry led an early attempt to reach the North Pole in 1827. This expedition travelled further north than any before it but did not reach the Pole. Frederick Cook claimed to have reached the Pole in 1908. But many consider an expedition led by the American Robert Peary to have been the first to conquer it in 1909—even though some scholars think Peary's records do not provide enough support for the claim. In 1926, Roald Amundsen flew over the North Pole in the airship *Norge* and the first crossing under the Pole in a submarine was made by the U.S.S. *Nautilus* in 1958.

ARCTIC EXPLORATION

Before Peary's successful 1909 North Pole attempt, other expeditions had ventured into the Arctic Ocean. Several ended in tragedy, such as John Franklin's 1845 expedition.

Peary, 1909

Franklin, 1845

Peary, 1909
This map shows Peary's route to the North Pole—his fourth attempt. From their base on Ellesmere Island, the journey to the Pole took 37 days.

Franklin, 1845
Franklin attempted to map the Northwest Passage between the Atlantic and Pacific oceans. He and his team were last seen in Lancaster Sound and expedition remains were found on Beechey Island five years later.

Final team
This photo by Robert Peary shows his five-man team that reached the North Pole. The team included four skilled Inuit sledge drivers—Ooqeah, Ootah, Egingwah and Seeglo—and fellow American Matthew Henson.

Greenland huskies *Around 200 huskies were transported from Smith Sound, Greenland, for the expedition. Five to seven of these extremely powerful dogs were used to pull each sledge.*

Sealskin clothing *The Inuit on Peary's expedition had important skills for surviving the cold. These included making the traditional, lightweight and warm fur clothing used by Peary and his men.*

Low sledge *Peary designed and Henson built the expedition sledges that carried food, fuel and other supplies. They were made of wood and had steel runners.*

Wooden skis *The skis used by early polar explorers were made of wood. Peary's expedition used skis when the surface of the snow suited them.*

Final dash

On 1 March 1909, 24 men driving 19 sledges pulled by 130 huskies set out on the Arctic sea ice. Along the route to the Pole, Robert Peary had carefully planned support teams to set up depots of supplies and build igloos. When they were 246 kilometres (153 mi) from the Pole, Peary, Matthew Henson and four Inuit left the last of the support parties behind and made the final dash for the Pole. They arrived at the North Pole on 6 April 1909.

Dangerous Expeditions South
Endurance

Since it was first sighted in 1819, people have journeyed south to learn about the Antarctic continent. The most famous were the explorers of the "Heroic Age" between 1900 and 1916. Frostbite and scurvy stopped Robert Falcon Scott's first attempt to reach the South Pole in 1902. Ernest Shackleton led another attempt in 1908 but, exhausted and short of food, he and his three companions had to turn back less than 160 kilometres (100 mi) from the Pole. A Norwegian team led by Roald Amundsen became the first to reach the South Pole in December 1911, followed closely by Scott. In 1914, Shackleton set out to cross the Antarctic continent from one side to the other, but his ship became trapped in pack ice.

Trapped in ice

In 1914, Shackleton and 27 men set sail aboard the *Endurance* for Antarctica. Within sight of the continent, the ship became trapped in pack ice. It drifted north for months and was finally crushed by the ice in October 1915. The men managed to save supplies and equipment from the ship. A dramatic escape and rescue adventure followed and miraculously all the men on the expedition were rescued.

SCOTT'S LAST EXPEDITION

In January 1912, Scott and four companions arrived at the South Pole to find that Amundsen had beaten them to their goal. Tragedy struck on their return journey. First Evans died. Then, severely frostbitten, Oates left the party in a storm. Scott, Wilson and Bowers struggled on until they were caught in a terrible blizzard and died.

Heavy sledges
Amundsen used dogs to pull his sledges. Scott and his men pulled all their equipment on their sledges themselves. It is a technique called "man-hauling" that takes an enormous amount of energy and strength.

Race to the South Pole
Scott's expedition to the South Pole started at Cape Evans, crossing the Ross Ice Shelf and Beardmore Glacier to the continent. Amundsen forged a new route to the Pole from a base camp 37 kilometres (60 mi) closer to the Pole.

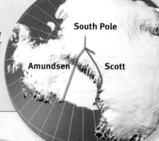

South Pole

Amundsen   Scott

Camp site *After spending winter aboard the* Endurance, *Shackleton and his men had to camp for six months on the pack ice before attempting to escape to Elephant Island.*

Crushing pressure *After the first winter, pressure from the pack ice grew in spring. It twisted the ship and caused it to tilt. Water rushed in, the decks broke upwards, and the ship had to be abandoned.*

Incredible lifeboat escape

After *Endurance* sank under the ice the crew were stranded on the pack ice. All 28 men managed to escape to land in three lifeboats. But Elephant Island, the land they escaped to, was remote and uninhabited. Shackleton and five men then set sail in the lifeboat the *James Caird* to South Georgia to find help. Returning to Elephant Island aboard a steam tug boat, Shackleton rescued all his men.

Elephant Island

South Georgia

Ice Shelf

Antarctica

— Route of the *James Caird*
— Escape in three lifeboats
•••• Route of the *Endurance*

Escape effort *Men with ice chisels tried to break up the ice while the engines were used at full speed to push through it, but without success. The ship was stuck.*

Safety lifeboat *Shortly after arriving at Elephant Island, Shackleton and five men set off on a 1,290 kilometres (800 mi) journey aboard the James Caird lifeboat. The boat was just 7 metres (23 ft) long. They arrived in South Georgia 16 days later.*

ENDURANCE

Warm and Dry
Clothing

Humans maintain a core body temperature at around 37°C (98.6°F). When exposed to extreme cold, our body loses heat faster than it is produced, and can reach a temperature too low to function normally. This condition is called hypothermia—in the most severe cases it leads to death. Other animals have fur, blubber or feathers to trap heat, but people must rely on clothing to keep them warm. It must also keep them dry, because wet clothes sap warmth away from the body. Traditionally, polar clothing is made from the fur of animals such as reindeers and polar bears. Today, synthetic and natural materials are used in polar clothing.

Eye protection
Bright sunlight reflected off snow and ice can cause loss of vision, called snow blindness. The small slits in Inuit snow goggles (above) and the tinted lenses of modern goggles (below) limit the amount of light that reaches the eyes.

Furry hood *Like the traditional Inuit parka, the hood is trimmed with fur. Your breath contains water vapour that freezes in cold air. Fur around the hood sheds any ice that forms on it and keeps snow out of the face.*

Multi-layered *Next to the skin, a long-sleeved vest made of soft, synthetic fabric draws away moisture from sweat. Shirts, fleeces and woollen jumpers provide layers of insulation. The outer parka layer is both water and windproof.*

Jacket and hood *This parka jacket is made from reindeer skin. The hood is important as 20–40 per cent of all heat lost by a person is through their head. Underneath this thick fur coat, a softer layer of underclothes is worn.*

Outer and inner gloves *Under the thick outer mittens, thinner inner gloves are usually worn, so that the mittens can be removed without exposing the hands to cold air.*

Synthetic trousers *A thick, warm pair of trousers is worn over thermal longjohns. A waterproof, windproof outer layer is worn over the these.*

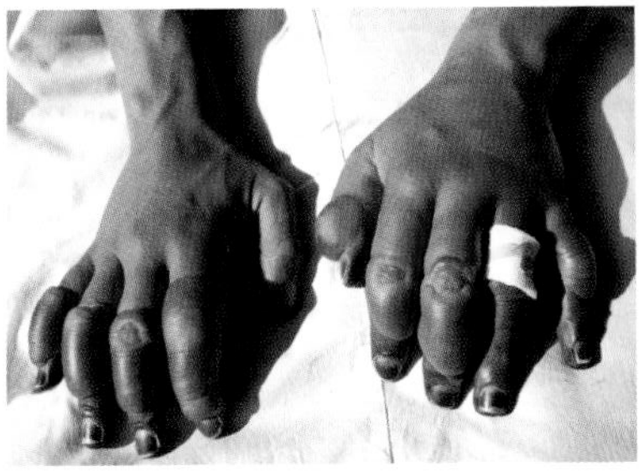

Water

Moisture from sweating

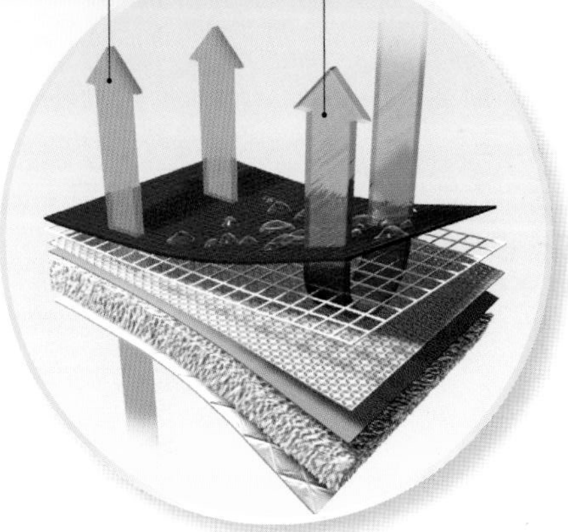

Modern materials

Modern synthetic fabrics are often used in polar clothing. One example is GORE-TEX®, which is waterproof and breathable. This allows moisture from sweating to escape but does not let water in, keeping the wearer dry.

"Mukluk" boots *"Mukluk" boots have a thick rubber sole and layers to keep the feet warm. They are good on hard, dry snow. However, skiing, mountaineering and walking on wet snow all require different footwear.*

Fur boots *Several layers are worn on the feet to keep them warm. The outer layer is usually made of reindeer or seal skin.*

Fur mittens *It is essential to protect hands from the cold as they can be damaged by frostbite in minutes. Mittens made from fur, often seal skin, keep hands warm.*

Fur trousers *Trousers are also made from fur, often reindeer or polar bear skin.*

Frostbite

In extreme cold, the skin and other tissues can freeze—called frostbite. This usually affects hands and feet as they are furthest from the warm core of the body. Skin turns black and nerves and blood vessels may be damaged.

Polar clothes

This illustration shows traditional clothing worn by the Inuit in the Arctic (left), and clothing worn by modern polar explorers and scientists (right). In traditional Arctic clothing, fur is carefully hand-stitched together. It is lightweight and a superb insulator, trapping air to stop heat from escaping. In modern polar clothing, many layers trap air between them, while allowing moisture to escape.

Shelter
Keeping the Cold Outside

The polar regions are the coldest places on Earth. Humans must build shelters to survive the cold, snow, wind and, at times, the wildlife. In the Arctic, most Inuit now live in timber houses in villages. But they still build their famous igloos—domed structures of snow blocks—as temporary shelters when on winter hunting trips. The early explorers of Antarctica built huts from timber they took with them. Some huts still stand, more than 100 years later. Today, scientists working in Antarctica stay on research bases that are constructed using the latest materials and engineering techniques. Out in the field, they camp in pyramid tents designed to withstand the ferocious Antarctic winds.

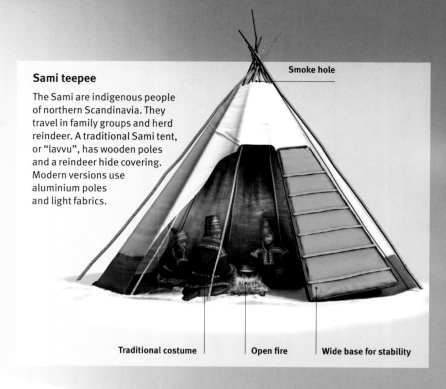

Sami teepee
The Sami are indigenous people of northern Scandinavia. They travel in family groups and herd reindeer. A traditional Sami tent, or "lavvu", has wooden poles and a reindeer hide covering. Modern versions use aluminium poles and light fabrics.

Smoke hole

Traditional costume | Open fire | Wide base for stability

INSIDE AN IGLOO

Igloo life
An igloo is quite cosy inside. Stoves are sometimes used for cooking. This can cause the blocks to melt a little, but the moisture freezes overnight, making the dome even stronger.

Roof pattern
The dome roof does not need any poles to keep it up. With its spiral of blocks, the dome supports itself and is very strong.

Building an igloo

An igloo is a dome built from blocks of hard, wind-compacted snow. The blocks are placed in a spiral pattern, each one tilted slightly inwards. This makes a very stable structure. Once the dome and the entrance tunnel are complete, any gaps between the blocks are filled in with loose snow. Snow is a good insulator, so it can be quite warm inside.

Modern clothing *Traditional Inuit clothes are made from animal skins. These days, the Inuit often wear modern manufactured clothing, too.*

Shaping snow *Blocks are cut out of hard snow using an ice saw. Each block is shaped to fit tightly against the other blocks.*

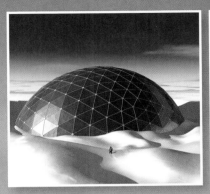

Dome research station
The dome of the American Amundsen–Scott South Pole Station was built in the early 1970s. It had to close because the weight of snow cover weakened the dome.

Hydraulic lift station
The new building sits on huge hydraulic jacks, which can raise it two storeys to stay above the snow. The wind can also blow snow out from under the building.

Placing blocks *Before a block is put in place, its edges are rubbed with the ice saw. This melts the snow a little. It freezes again when the block is in place, forming a strong join.*

Entrance tunnel *The floor of the entrance tunnel is often dug out. This makes it possible to get in and out with only a small opening to the outside.*

Finding Food

Hunting

Most of the land in Polar Regions lies under a thick blanket of snow for much of the year. Arctic peoples have survived on the produce of these frozen lands for thousands of years. In summer, bilberries and cranberries provide important vitamins, and eggs are collected from sea bird colonies. In winter, meat forms the main part of the diet. Seal and reindeer meat are most commonly eaten, but larger animals such as polar bears and bowhead whales are also hunted for food. Antarctica has no indigenous peoples. Researchers in Antarctica eat a balanced diet that has been carefully planned by scientists. Some Antarctic stations even have greenhouses to produce fresh fruit and vegetables.

Traditional hunting *An Inuit has dropped a fishing line down through a hole in the ice. The sinker at the end of the line weighs it down. Sinkers were often carved from whalebone or walrus ivory.*

Seafood *Ling cod, Arctic char and halibut are important in the diet of the Inuit. They are high in protein and provide vitamins and minerals. Inuit also eat shrimp, krill and other crustaceans.*

Food in the sea
The ecosystem under the sea ice supports much of the life above it. Traditionally, the Inuit fish through holes in the ice, or wait to harpoon seals surfacing at breathing holes. In open water, larger prey such as bowhead whales and narwhals are hunted. On land, musk oxen and polar bears are prey to hunters using spears or bows and arrows. Arctic peoples have great respect for the animals they hunt and believe that they have spirits.

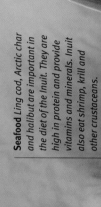

Ling cod

Ringed seal

Shrimp

Explorer diet
Explorers take most of their food with them on expeditions. This photo shows food for one man for one day from the Scott Antarctic expedition, 1910–1912. Pemmican, a mixture of meat, animal fat and dried fruit, formed much of the diet of early Antarctic explorers.

HANDCRAFTED TOOLS

Traditional Inuit hunting tools are made from bone, animal hide and walrus ivory. Spears are used to catch fish, and harpoons to catch seals and whales. The head of a harpoon comes off when wedged in the flesh of the animal.

Fishing spear

Knife used in preparing food

Harpoon head

Detachable harpoon heads

Whale To catch a whale requires teamwork—men to keep the boat steady and men to spear the whale. Large floats are attached to the harpoons to stop the whale from sinking. Whale skin contains vitamin C and is eaten, along with the meat.

Seal Seals form a large part of the traditional Inuit diet. As well as protein, seal meat contains vitamin A and iron. Seal blubber is used as fuel, and their skins, with their warm fur, are made into clothing.

Bowhead whale

Common minke whale

Poles in Danger

Threats

Burning fossil fuels such as coal and oil is leading to an
increase in the amount of carbon dioxide in the atmosphere.
Carbon dioxide is a greenhouse gas that traps the Sun's
energy and causes Earth's climate to get warmer. Without
greenhouse gases Earth would be too cold for life to survive,
but the huge amount of carbon dioxide being released by
human activities is pushing Earth's climate out of balance.
The rising temperatures are causing major changes to the
polar regions. Polar sea ice is decreasing, and a global rise
in temperature of just 1.5°C (34.7°F) could cause the second
largest ice sheet in the world, the Greenland ice sheet, to shrink.

Clear passage *The Northwest Passage is a route ships can use between the Atlantic and Pacific oceans through the Arctic Ocean, north of Canada. In 2007, sea ice decreased so much, it became ice-free for the first time since satellite records began in 1978.*

OZONE HOLE

The ozone layer absorbs the Sun's harmful
ultraviolet radiation. Over time pollutants have
thinned the concentration of ozone over the globe
and most visibly over Antarctica during early spring.

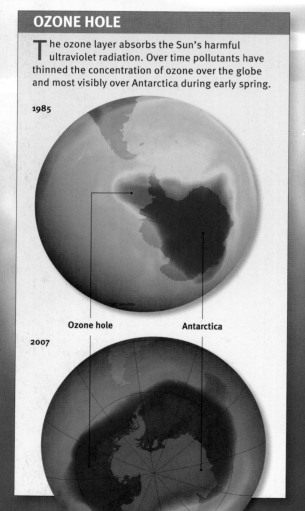

1985

Ozone hole   Antarctica

2007

Endangered ecosystems *Rising temperatures are affecting Arctic ecosystems from algae up to the top predators. Polar bears live and hunt on the sea ice. They now have to swim further to find ice platforms from which they can hunt.*

Melting Arctic

Temperatures in the Arctic are rising almost twice as fast as the average global temperature. This is already having a major effect on Arctic sea ice. Sea ice is thinner than it used to be, and satellite images show us dramatic changes in its surface area. In the summer of 2007, sea ice covered just 4.2 million square kilometres (1.6 million sq mi) of the Arctic Ocean, compared to 7.8 million square kilometres (3 million sq mi) in the summer of 1980.

Changing environment *Frozen habitats are decreasing and species from warmer climates are starting to invade. Warming of the polar regions could lead to major changes to the circulation of the oceans, affecting climates, wildlife and people worldwide.*

Melting Ice
Polar Future

Most scientists agree that human activities are leading to an increase in global temperatures. Temperatures are rising most rapidly in polar regions, with major consequences for climates and ecosystems worldwide. The polar icecaps store huge amounts of water. The Antarctic ice sheet holds 70 per cent of the world's fresh water. If this were to melt completely, sea levels would rise by 70 metres (230 ft). This is unlikely to happen, and would take thousands of years at current warming rates. But a number of scientific studies predict significant sea level rises by 2100, which would affect billions of people worldwide, particularly those in developing countries.

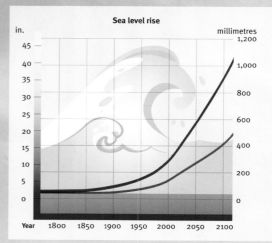

Sea level rise

If sea levels continue rising at their current rate, they could be about 480 millimetres (19 in) higher by 2100, shown with an orange line. Further global warming and loss of ice from ice sheets in Greenland or Antarctica could push this level even higher to 1,000 millimetres (39 in) shown in the graph with a green line.

Vulnerable coastline *Storms cause huge swells in the ocean, which can flood coastal areas. Increased sea levels make these surges more severe, and the chances of flooding more likely.*

Warming oceans *Sea level rise is not just caused by more water from melting ice sheets. As the planet warms, the water of the oceans expands.*

CLUES IN THE ICE

Drilled from ice sheets and glaciers, an ice core is a cylinder of ice, sometimes kilometres in length. At its base, it can be thousands of years old. Chemical analysis of the ice, and air trapped within it, have shown a positive link between temperature and the amount of carbon dioxide in the atmosphere.

Rising seas

With hundreds of miles of coastline, New York City is vulnerable to flooding from sea level rise. The image here shows New York under 10 metres (33 ft) of water. This sea level rise is unlikely in the near future, but even a small increase would make flooding from storm surges more frequent and severe. This would cause damage to homes, businesses and transport networks. New York will have to adapt by building flood defences and by eventually moving to higher ground.

Flooded economies *Poorer developing countries will struggle the most with sea level rise, such as in Bangladesh where 80–90 per cent of the country is less than one metre (3.3 ft) above sea level.*

Salty land *Seawater is salty. As sea levels rise, this salt water would travel further inland, affecting soils, crops and habitats. It could also threaten human water supplies.*

City life *Innovative houses that float on water could be built and the use of boats for transport increase if sea levels rise.*

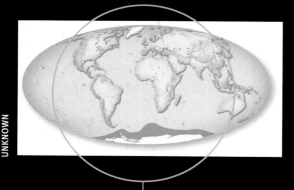

LEOPARD SEAL: THE FACTS

SPECIES: *Hydrurga leptonyx*

GROUP: Mammals

DIET: Krill, fish, penguins, seabirds and other seals, particularly crabeater seals

HABITAT: Ocean and pack ice around Antarctica; can be found as far north as Australia

REPRODUCTION: Females give birth to 1 pup in November–December every year, from the age of 6 years

LIFE EXPECTANCY: Around 26 years

Fast facts Fast facts at your fingertips give you essential information about the animal species featured.

Locator map The green shading on this map of the world shows you where the featured animal lives.

Extinction risk This bar shows which category the animal belongs to.

in *focus*

GREY WOLF: THE FACTS

SPECIES: *Canis lupus*

GROUP: Mammals

DIET: Caribou, musk oxen and moose, also smaller animals such as beavers and Arctic hare

HABITAT: All land habitats except arid desert and tropical forest

REPRODUCTION: Only the alpha pair mate. The alpha female gives birth to a litter of 5–14 pups each year

LIFE EXPECTANCY: 10 years

Stiff tail *The tail shows rank within a pack. A dominant wolf holds its tail stiff and upright; a submissive animal holds its tail between its legs. A wolf also expresses its mood with its tail, wagging it when happy.*

10-year-old boy
1.4 m (4.5 ft)

Male grey wolf
1 m (3.3 ft)

Body Language
Grey Wolf

Grey wolves are found in North America, Europe and Asia, from the Arctic in the north to as far south as Mexico. However, these large carnivores have disappeared from many areas because of hunting. People often fear wolves but despite their grisly reputation, wolves rarely attack humans. Grey wolves vary in size—the largest wolves are found in the north. They also vary in colour, from grey-brown fur to almost black, and white wolves live in the Arctic tundra. Wolves use facial expressions, body language and sounds to communicate with each other. They howl to let other members of a pack know where they are, when they are hunting or defending their territory.

Pack hunters

Wolves often hunt large prey, such as caribou, moose and musk oxen. These animals can be dangerous. Although individual wolves can attack on their own, they usually hunt such large prey as a pack.

1 Stalking Wolves use many cues to find prey, including scent and visual information. Once prey is located, they get as close as possible without being seen.

2 Panic Wolves chase prey and make them run so they can find the weakest members of the herd to attack—in this case it is the caribou calf.

3 Capture The caribou are confused. The calf runs in the opposite direction to its mother and is caught by the wolves.

UNKNOWN

LOWER RISK

VULNERABLE

ENDANGERED

High hackles *When showing aggressive or dominant behaviour, the hairs on the back of a wolf's neck stand on end. These hairs are known as the wolf's hackles. Domestic dogs behave in a similar way.*

Leader of the pack

Wolves usually live in packs of between two and 40 animals. There is a clear pecking order in each pack of wolves. The alpha male and female are dominant— they eat first at a kill and are the only animals in the pack to breed. This wolf is displaying dominant behaviour. Lower ranking wolves show submissive behaviour, which can include crouching and holding their ears back and down.

Eye contact
A dominant animal looks a lower-ranking wolf in the eye.

Scary snarl *A wolf snarls to show its sharp teeth. Its snarl may be a sign dominance or aggression, or part of the wolf's self-defence.*

Terrifying teeth
A wolf's jaws are strong and its teeth are sharp. It uses its long, curved canines to grasp prey, while teeth further back in the mouth slice it into chunks that the wolf can swallow.

WOLF RELATIVES

The grey wolf is the largest member of the canid, or dog, family. Canids have long legs, a bushy tail and slender muzzle. They are found all over the world and include domestic dogs.

Coyote
The coyote is closely related to, but smaller than, the grey wolf. It is found across North and Central America, except in the far north of Canada.

Wolverine
Despite its name, the wolverine is not a member of the canid family. It is more closely related to stoats, weasels and otters than it is to dogs.

Arctic fox
The Arctic fox is a small predator found in the Arctic regions. Its muzzle, legs and ears are short compared to those of other canids.

MUSK OX: THE FACTS

SPECIES:	*Ovibos moschatus*
GROUP:	Mammals
DIET:	Grasses, reeds and sedges
HABITAT:	Arctic tundra
REPRODUCTION:	Females give birth to 1 calf, or occasionally twins, every year, from the age of around 2 years
LIFE EXPECTANCY:	20–24 years

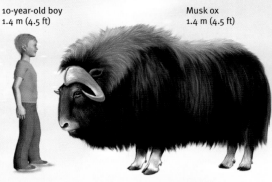

10-year-old boy
1.4 m (4.5 ft)

Musk ox
1.4 m (4.5 ft)

Defensive Huddle
Musk Ox

Musk oxen are herbivorous mammals, closely related to goats. They feed on grasses and other plants of the Arctic tundra. In the winter, they dig through the snow to get to their food, and usually stay on hilltops and slopes where stronger winds create shallower snow. Musk oxen are very sturdy, with hunched shoulders and a short neck and legs. Two large horns curve down and out from the skull of both males and females. Their dark brown fur has coarse guard hairs, which almost reach the ground, over a soft, dense underwool. Musk oxen usually live in herds of 10 to 20 animals, although herds of as many as 100 have been seen.

Musk gland *A small scent gland produces a musky odour, source of the oxen's common name. Males produce the smell during the rut, when they fight for dominance.*

Hoof *The hooves are large and round. They spread the weight of these big, heavy animals so they do not sink into the snow.*

UNKNOWN

LOWER RISK

VULNERABLE

ENDANGERED

Safety in numbers

Under attack from wolves, a herd of musk oxen huddles together in a circle or semicircle. The oxen face their attackers, presenting a wall of large, sharp horns. This defence works well against wolves, but it made musk oxen easy targets for human hunters. In the nineteenth century, the oxen were hunted for their fur, meat and horns, and were almost wiped out in Canada and Alaska. However, conservation efforts mean that musk oxen are roaming the Arctic tundra of North America once again.

Woolly coat *Long, coarse guard hairs shed water and snow to keep the coat dry. The thick, soft underwool insulates against the Arctic winter; it falls out in spring.*

DEFENSIVE CIRCLE

When threatened, musk oxen form a defensive circle, facing outward to confront their attacker. Calves are most vulnerable, so they stay inside the circle, behind the adults with their huge horns.

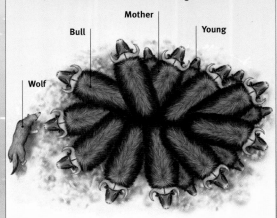

Mother
Bull
Young
Wolf

Horns *The horns start growing when a calf is 4–5 weeks old. Males have the biggest horns. They are used in dominance battles and against predators.*

Spiny palate *The palate is covered with spines to grip slippery fish. This allows puffins to catch up to 12 small fish in a trip.*

Colourful beak *The beak is brightly coloured only in the breeding season. Its outer shell is lost in winter, and the beak looks smaller and duller.*

ATLANTIC PUFFIN: THE FACTS

SPECIES: *Fratercula arctica*

GROUP: Birds

DIET: Small fish, such as sand eels, and other marine animals, such as squid and crustaceans

HABITAT: North Atlantic based; spend much of their life on the water; breed on islands, nesting in large colonies

REPRODUCTION: Females lay 1 egg each year, from the age of around 4–5 years; the chick is reared by both parents

LIFE EXPECTANCY: 20 years

Inside a Nest

Atlantic Puffin

Atlantic puffins are small seabirds that live along the coasts of northern Europe, Greenland, Iceland and northeastern North America. They are easy to recognise in summer, with their striking black and white plumage and bright orange beak. In winter, the beak loses its colourful outer sheath and dark feathers grow over the white face patches. Puffins need to eat more than 40 fish a day to survive and are adapted to life on the water. But pollution is affecting this marine habitat. Also, cats and rats have been introduced on some of their breeding islands and prey on the puffin colonies there.

BODY MOVEMENT

Puffins are expert swimmers and divers, well adapted to spending much of the year at sea. However, they breed on land, and they also fly.

Swimming
Puffins use their wings in a flying motion to swim through the water. Their large webbed feet steer.

Flying
Puffins can fly short distances. To stay airborne, their wings beat 5–6 times a second. They fly into the wind to land.

Underground nest

Puffins nest in burrows as long as 2 metres (6.6 ft) in the ground. Sometimes they use old rabbit burrows, or they dig a burrow themselves with their beaks and feet. Inside the burrow, the female lays a single large egg. Both parents take it in turns to incubate the egg, and after about 40 days it hatches. The parents fly out to sea to bring food back for the chick. Around 43 days after hatching, the chick starts to spend time outside the burrow. One week later, it fledges and is independent.

10-year-old boy
1.4 m (4.5 ft)

Male puffin
0.2 m (0.7 ft)

Chick Adult puffins feed their chicks beakfuls of fish. The adult feathers of this two-week-old chick develop underneath its downy brown feathers.

UNKNOWN

LOWER RISK

VULNERABLE

ENDANGERED

POLAR BEAR: THE FACTS

SPECIES: *Ursus maritimus*

GROUP: **Mammals**

DIET: Seals, belugas, narwhals, fish, sea birds, reindeer, some vegetation such as berries (known to hunt humans)

HABITAT: Sea ice and coast around the Arctic Ocean

REPRODUCTION: Females give birth to a litter of 1–4 cubs every 2–4 years, from the age of around 5–6 years

LIFE EXPECTANCY: 25–30 years

10-year-old boy
1.4 m (4.5 ft)

Male polar bear
1.6 m (5.2 ft)

Underground Den
Polar Bear

Huge and powerful, polar bears are the top predators in the Arctic and the world's largest land-living carnivores. They are well insulated from the cold with thick fur and blubber. Their fur has both water-repellent guard hairs and soft, dense underfur. Polar bears live on and around the sea ice and they mostly hunt ringed and bearded seals. When they hunt, polar bears often wait next to holes in the sea ice used by seals to breathe. But they also stalk their prey on the surface of the ice. One of the biggest threats to polar bears is climate change, which is reducing the amount of sea ice on which the bears can hunt. Some populations of polar bears have already begun to decline.

Sense of smell *Polar bears can smell seals and other polar bears from as far as 5 kilometres (3 mi) away. Males are much larger than females and are known to feed on cubs.*

Entrance tunnel *When the cubs are ready to go outside, the mother breaks through the entrance of the tunnel. The family stays close to the den for around 15 days before journeying to the pack ice to hunt.*

Keeping warm
When temperatures are very low, polar bears curl up, covering their nose. The snow that collects on their body helps insulate them from the cold.

Resting, sleeping and wandering 81%

Hunting 19%

SPRING

Resting, sleeping and wandering 62%

Hunting 38%

SUMMER

Mother and cub activity
Scientists watch and record polar bear activity. These pie charts show how a female and her cubs spend their time in the spring (March, April and May) and summer (June, July and August).

Inside the den

In the autumn, a pregnant female polar bear digs her maternity den. Inside, she gives birth to a litter of cubs that are small and blind, and have only a thin layer of fur. They all remain in the den, protected from the cold Arctic winter, until the following spring. While in the den the mother does not feed, but provides the cubs with fat-rich milk.

Breathing hole *This hole allows air exchange between the den and the outside world. It is often covered by snowfall.*

Conserving energy *The mother enters a state similar to hibernation. Her reduced heart rate uses less energy, which is vital as it could be eight months until she eats again.*

LARGE PADDED PAWS

The very large paws of polar bears spread the enormous weight of the animal over a wide area. This stops them from sinking into the snow. A layer of fur on the soles of their feet also helps insulate the paws against the cold ice.

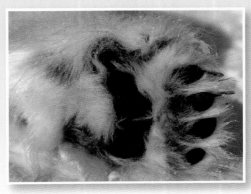

Heat absorber
The pads on the soles of the paws are black—the colour of polar bear skin. Dark surfaces absorb more heat, so having dark skin helps polar bears to keep warm.

Playful cubs *A polar bear litter usually contains two cubs, but there can be up to four young. Cubs stay in their family group until around the age of two.*

UNKNOWN

LOWER RISK

VULNERABLE

ENDANGERED

Jawbone

Flexible neck *The neck is narrow and, unlike many whales and dolphins, individual neck vertebrae are not fused together. This means that belugas are able to nod and turn their heads from side to side.*

Malleable melon *The melon is a structure filled with oil that gives the beluga's forehead its bulging appearance. A beluga can change the shape of its melon, perhaps to help make noises and the clicks for echolocation.*

Nasal sacs

Dorsal ridge *Belugas do not have the dorsal fin typical of many whales and dolphins. Instead, they have a low ridge running along their back, which may be an adaptation for swimming beneath sea ice.*

BELUGA: THE FACTS

SPECIES: *Delphinapterus leucas*

GROUP: Mammals

DIET: Fish and marine invertebrates

HABITAT: Coastal and deep waters of the Arctic Ocean and adjoining seas

REPRODUCTION: From the age of around 5 years onwards, a female beluga gives birth to a single calf every 3 years

LIFE EXPECTANCY: Uncertain, but possibly 25–35 years

White Whale

Beluga

The white whale, or beluga, is a small toothed whale found in the Arctic Ocean and neighbouring seas. Belugas are dark grey at birth. As they grow, they lighten to their creamy white adult colour by reducing the amount of the pigment melanin in their skin. Belugas use whistles, chirps and squeals to communicate with each other. They are nicknamed "sea canaries" because of the noises they make. Some noises are so loud they can be heard above the surface of the water and through the hulls of boats. Belugas are prey to polar bears, orcas and people, who hunt them for their meat, skin and blubber. In some areas of the Arctic belugas have all but disappeared. Efforts are being made to control hunting and protect this species from extinction.

Social swimmers

Belugas generally live in small family groups, called pods, of up to 20 whales. However, during migrations and in places where food is particularly abundant, they can gather in schools of 10,000 animals. Different populations of belugas have different migratory patterns, depending on available food and the distribution of pack ice. Some do not migrate at all, staying in the same area all year round.

10-year-old boy
1.4 m (4.5 ft)

Beluga
4 m (13 ft)

Beluga calf
1.6 m (5,3 ft)

Ornate tail *The base of the tail is narrow, and its fin is broad and curved with a central notch. As a beluga ages, its tail becomes more curved and ornate.*

NARWHAL

The narwhal is an Arctic whale closely related to the beluga. It feeds on fish, squid and shrimp. Narwhals swim in groups of 15–20 animals, though hundreds can congregate together. The function of the narwhal's tusk is poorly understood by scientists.

Big tooth
The narwhal's tusk is a greatly extended left incisor tooth up to 3 metres (10 ft) long. It usually only grows in males. Occasionally, dual-tusked narwhals are found, where another tusk has developed from a right incisor.

WALRUS: THE FACTS

SPECIES: *Odobenus rosmarus*

GROUP: Mammals

DIET: Clams, mussels and other invertebrates (animals without backbones) from the seafloor

HABITAT: Pack ice in the Arctic Ocean

REPRODUCTION: Females give birth to a maximum of 1 calf every 2 years, from the age of 6 years

LIFE EXPECTANCY: 40 years

10-year-old boy
1.4 m (4.5 ft)

Male walrus
1.5 m (4.9 ft) high

1-year-old calf
0.5 m (1.5 ft) high

Threatening Tusks

Walrus

Walruses are large marine mammals. With their thick blubber, wrinkled skin and moustache of stout whiskers, they look like the old men of the sea. Their most distinctive feature is their tusks, which are specially adapted canine teeth. Walruses live on the pack ice of the Arctic Ocean but are also perfectly at home in the water. They can even sleep there—inflatable pouches on either side of their head stop them from slipping below the surface. Many walruses migrate, following the sea ice as it expands south during the winter, then shrinks north in the summer. Thousands will haul themselves out of the water at certain beaches and lie close together in huge colonies.

FORAGING FOR FOOD

Walruses forage on the seafloor at 10–50 metres (33–164 ft) deep. By squirting jets of water from their mouth, they stir up sediment to help reveal clams and other prey. They suck the clams out of the shells.

Fore flipper *When swimming, the front flippers paddle or are held in against the body. The flipper soles are rough to stop the walrus slipping on the ice.*

Male rivals

Walruses use their tusks to compete against each other for dominance. They will throw back their head to display their tusks and may even strike their rival with them. The dominant walruses are larger and their longer tusks can grow to more than 1 metre (3.3 ft). They get to use the best landing sites on the beach and have access to females to mate with.

Hind flipper *The rear flippers propel the walrus through the water. On land, the walrus can bring the flippers under its body and walk on all fours.*

Useful tusks *Tusks are mostly for dominance displays. They are also used in fights with predators, or as ice picks to help the walrus haul itself out of the sea onto the ice.*

Sensitive whiskers *Around 450 stiff, nerve-rich bristles cover the snout. They help detect food in the sediment on the murky ocean floor.*

Inside a tusk
Tusks are formed from dentine, and they keep growing all through the walrus's life. The core has a mottled appearance. The surrounding layers have faint lines that radiate outwards.

ORCA: THE FACTS

SPECIES: *Orcinus orca*

GROUP: Mammals

DIET: Seals, sea lions, walruses, other whales, fish, squid and seabirds

HABITAT: All the world's oceans; often prefer coastal areas

REPRODUCTION: Females give birth to 1 calf every 3–8 years, from the age of around 12 years

LIFE EXPECTANCY: Males to 60 years; females to 90 years

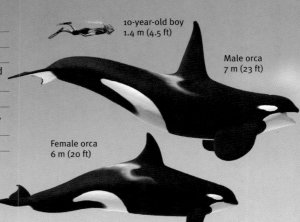

10-year-old boy
1.4 m (4.5 ft)

Male orca
7 m (23 ft)

Female orca
6 m (20 ft)

UNKNOWN

LOWER RISK

VULNERABLE

ENDANGERED

Killer Whale

Orca

Orcas are the largest members of the dolphin family and live in all the world's oceans. Males are bigger than females, and can grow up to 9.8 metres (32 ft) long. Size and strength make orcas very fast, while their throat is big enough to swallow a seal or small walrus whole. As the world's largest predators of warm-blooded prey, they have been given another name, "killer whales". Orcas are very social animals that produce whistles and other sounds to communicate with each other. They make clicking sounds to locate prey. Although orcas are not endangered, some populations are threatened by human activities such as overfishing and poison and oil spills.

Dorsal fin *A triangle-shaped dorsal fin is in the middle of the back. The female's dorsal fin is much smaller than the male's and curves further backwards.*

Pod *Orcas travel in pods. These family groups usually contain a large male, a large female, several smaller females and calves. Pods can join together into schools of 250 whales.*

Tempting meal *In the Antarctic some orcas mostly eat seals and fur seals. Some prefer minke whales. Others mostly feed on Antarctic toothfish.*

SPYHOPPING

Orcas can hold their bodies vertically with their heads above water, beating their tails to keep steady. This is called "spyhopping". It allows them to look around above the surface, possibly for prey.

Hunting tool *Orcas have 10 to 14 pointed teeth on either side of the jaw. They either swallow food whole or rip larger prey into chunks with these teeth.*

Stealth and speed

An orca surges onto a beach to snatch a fur seal pup from the surf. Orcas have many hunting techniques. They can flip over ice floes to get at the penguins above. They can break through a sheet of ice up to 1 metre (3.3 ft) thick by swimming upwards at speed. Sometimes orcas hunt in groups, tackling prey as big as blue whales.

ENDANGERED   VULNERABLE   LOWER RISK   UNKNOWN

High-speed Swimmer
Emperor Penguin

Emperor penguins are the largest of the world's 17 penguin species. They live on the pack ice fringing Antarctica, and hunt for squid, krill and fish in the Southern Ocean. From March to April they journey across the sea ice to breeding grounds, gathering in colonies of up to 25,000 pairs. Each female lays a large egg, passes it to her mate and then returns to the sea to feed. The males hold their egg on their feet and huddle together against the freezing Antarctic winter. When the chicks hatch, they eat a milky substance from their father until the mother returns a month later with regurgitated fish. The chicks begin to fledge and hunt 150 days after hatching.

EMPEROR PENGUIN: THE FACTS

SPECIES: *Aptenodytes forsteri*

GROUP: Birds

DIET: Fish, krill and squid

HABITAT: Sea ice and Southern Ocean around Antarctica

REPRODUCTION: Females lay 1 egg each year in May–June, from the age of 3 years; after almost 4 months of the father's care, the chick is reared by both parents

LIFE EXPECTANCY: 20 years

Built to swim

Although they cannot fly and look clumsy on land, emperor penguins are master swimmers. Their streamlined bodies pass through the water like a bullet to flee leopard seals and orcas. They can dive to 500 metres (1,640 ft) deep and stay underwater for up to 22 minutes. Their outer feathers are oiled, flat and watertight. This keeps them dry—wet feathers in such a cold environment would quickly chill and freeze their bodies.

Countershading *Looking up at a swimming penguin, its white belly is difficult to make out against the light at the surface. Looking down from above, its black back blends in with the dark ocean below.*

GETTING AROUND

Emperor penguins spend a lot of time in the water. They must also get around on the ice, especially on their annual journey to breed.

Tobogganing
Penguins slide around the ice on their bellies by pushing with their wings and feet.

Entering water
Penguins slide off the ice on their stomachs, entering the water in groups as protection from waiting predators.

Walking
Short legs and a thick body create a waddling walk. This walk uses twice as much energy as the walk of other land animals of a similar size.

Flipper wings *The wings are stiff, slender flippers that act like paddles in the water. Although penguins cannot fly, their swimming looks like underwater flying.*

10-year-old boy
1.4 metres
(4.5 ft)

Chinstrap penguin
68 centimetres
(2.2 ft)

King penguin
94 centimetres
(3 ft)

Rockhopper penguin
56 centimetres
(1.8 ft)

Emperor penguin
1.2 metres
(4 ft)

Adélie penguin
71 centimetres
(2.3 ft)

UNKNOWN

LOWER RISK

VULNERABLE

ENDANGERED

COLOSSAL SQUID: THE FACTS

SPECIES: *Mesonychoteuthis hamiltoni*

GROUP: Cephalopod mollusc

DIET: Fish, other squid and marine worms

HABITAT: Oceans around Antarctica; depth 1,000 metres (3,280 ft) or greater

REPRODUCTION: Little known; they probably lay eggs like other squid, from which small versions of adults hatch

LIFE EXPECTANCY: Unknown

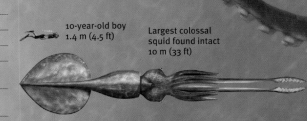

10-year-old boy 1.4 m (4.5 ft)

Largest colossal squid found intact 10 m (33 ft)

Giant of the Deep
Colossal Squid

Colossal squid are the world's largest invertebrates—animals without backbones. They live at depths of 1,000 metres (3,280 ft) or more. Only a few colossal squid have ever been found intact, so very little is known about them. The largest example, accidentally caught by fishermen in 2007, measured around 10 metres (33 ft) in length and weighed a massive 495 kilograms (1,089 lb). Larger body parts have been found in the stomachs of sperm whales. Scientists estimate that the maximum length for this species is 14 metres (46 ft). Colossal squid have highly developed senses and belong to the same species group as octopus and cuttlefish.

Balancing fins *The fins help to keep the animal steady in the water and are used to propel the squid forwards at slow speeds.*

ENORMOUS BODY

Colossal squid are huge. They have the largest eyes in the animal kingdom. If calamari rings were to be cut from a colossal squid, they would be about the size of truck tyres.

Squid eye

30 centimetres (12 in)

Calamari ring

90 centimetres (36 in)

Basketball

Truck tyre

High-speed swimmer

A squid uses jet propulsion to swim at high speeds, so that it can catch prey. A powerful muscle around the mantle of the squid tightens and forces a jet of water out through the underside of its body. This pushes it forwards through the water. The squid uses its arms and tentacles to capture prey and guide food to its beak.

Changing colour *Cells in the squid's skin contain a red pigment. These cells can contract and reduce the amount of red visible at the surface of the skin.*

Parrot

Colossal squid

Twin beaks

Colossal squid, like birds, have beaks made from very hard material. A squid uses its beak to slice up food into pieces small enough to eat.

Tentacle

Mantle *The mantle is a fold of skin that surrounds the main part of the body.*

Beak

Gripping arm *Each arm has hooks and toothed suckers. These help the squid hold onto its prey while it kills and eats it with its beak.*

Deadly club *At the end of both tentacles is a club. On the club are hooks that can rotate more than 360 degrees.*

LEOPARD SEAL: THE FACTS

SPECIES: *Hydrurga leptonyx*

GROUP: Mammals

DIET: Krill, fish, penguins, seabirds and other seals, particularly crabeater seals

HABITAT: Ocean and pack ice around Antarctica; can be found as far north as Australia

REPRODUCTION: Females give birth to 1 pup in November–December every year, from the age of 6 years

LIFE EXPECTANCY: Around 26 years

10-year-old boy
1.4 m (4.5 ft)

Male leopard seal
3 m (9.8 ft)

Fearsome Predator

Leopard Seal

With their spotted coat and fearsome hunting ability, leopard seals are truly leopards of the sea. They roam the oceans of Antarctica and are the only seals known to eat warm-blooded prey. Individual leopard seals often specialise in what they will hunt. Some are good at catching seal pups. Others specialise in penguins, patrolling the edge of the ice pack, and waiting for a penguin to dive into the water. The only animals to hunt and eat them are orcas. Leopard seals are solitary. They spend much of their lives alone in the ocean, except during the breeding season. Then they come on land in pairs or small groups. Both males and females sing, perhaps to find one another.

Furry pups
This harp seal pup's fur is thick and white for camouflage, like most seal pups. Leopard seal pups have fur the same colour as the adults'.

TWO TYPES OF SEAL

There are two groups of seal: eared seals, which include sea lions, and non-eared, or "true", seals, which include leopard seals. The "ear" refers to the outer ear flap, or pinna. True seals can hear.

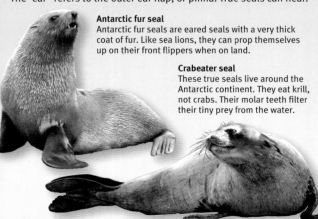

Antarctic fur seal
Antarctic fur seals are eared seals with a very thick coat of fur. Like sea lions, they can prop themselves up on their front flippers when on land.

Crabeater seal
These true seals live around the Antarctic continent. They eat krill, not crabs. Their molar teeth filter their tiny prey from the water.

Leopard spots *The coat is darker on top, paler underneath. Spots across the shoulders, throat and sides give these seals their name.*

UNKNOWN

LOWER RISK

VULNERABLE

ENDANGERED

Leopards of the sea

A leopard seal powers through the water, its streamlined body built for hunting at speed. It has a large head, enormous jaws and excellent senses of sight and smell. It uses its long, sharp canine teeth to capture large prey such as penguins. Then it thrashes the prey from side to side to rip it into pieces small enough to swallow. Its molar teeth, which are behind the canines, are not for chewing; they filter krill from the seawater.

Giant jaws *The long jaws open at a very wide angle. Powerful jaw-closing muscles and long canine teeth are important when capturing large prey.*

Fore flipper *These are very large and powerful. Leopard seals use their fore flippers to manoeuvre more than other true seals do.*

Three-cusped tooth *The molar teeth have a complicated shape with three sharp cusps, or points. The top and bottom molars lock together to sieve krill from the water. Although leopard seals are famous for eating penguins, krill make up 40 per cent of their diet.*

WANDERING ALBATROSS: THE FACTS

SPECIES: *Diomedea exulans*

GROUP: Birds

DIET: Fish, squid and carrion from the surface of the ocean

HABITAT: Flies over the open ocean, nests on subantarctic islands such as South Georgia

REPRODUCTION: Albatrosses breed from the age of around 9 years. Pairs raise at best a single chick every 2 years.

LIFE EXPECTANCY: Up to 80 years

10-year-old boy arm span 1.4 m (4.5 ft)

Snow petrel wingspan 60 cm (2 ft)

Snowy owl wingspan 1.5 m (5 ft)

Wandering albatross wingspan 3.5 m (11.5 ft)

Wandering
Albatross

The wandering albatross has the largest wingspan of any living bird. Its long, narrow wings are perfect for soaring and gliding over the open ocean. Albatrosses are so skilled at getting lift from the wind that they can fly for hours without a single wing-beat. They often fly continuously for months at a time, feeding on fish and squid on the ocean's surface. Albatrosses can cover 900 kilometres (560 mi) in just one day, flying at speeds of up to 80 kilometres per hour (50 mph). They come to land to breed, nesting in colonies on subantarctic islands. The wandering albatross is a threatened species, with long-line fishing lines accidentally trapping thousands of these magnificent birds each year.

Built for flight *Albatross wings are long and thin. When flying they are kept in an outstretched position by a special locking mechanism in the shoulder. This saves energy, as it means muscle power is not required to hold the wings horizontally.*

Flying machine

Most birds flap their wings to generate lift, but wandering albatrosses get all the lift they need from winds blowing across the Southern Ocean. This is largely down to their wing shape and size. However, long wings are not very manoeuvrable so flapping flight is difficult. Albatrosses have to take a run up when taking off to get enough lift to become airborne.

UNKNOWN

LOWER RISK

VULNERABLE

ENDANGERED

Hollow bones *Flying birds have hollow bones, and albatrosses are no exception. Bone is heavy, so hollow bones help keep the weight of the bird to a minimum.*

NEXT GENERATION

A single egg is laid in December or January and hatches in early March. The young albatross is fed regularly for the first 4–5 weeks, then its parents return at irregular intervals to feed it until it fledges in November or December.

Mud-pillar nest
Albatrosses build their nests from mud amongst tussocks of grass on windy island slopes. They have one mate for life, and pairs return to the same nest site to raise each new chick.

Muscle power *Muscles in the breast provide power for flapping flight. This is important in take off, but once airborne an albatross rarely needs to flap its wings.*

BLUE WHALE: THE FACTS

SPECIES: *Balaenoptera musculus*

GROUP: Mammals

DIET: Krill and other small marine invertebrates

HABITAT: Oceans

REPRODUCTION: Females give birth to 1 calf every 2–3 years, from the age of around 10 years; gestation is 12 months

LIFE EXPECTANCY: Estimated to 110 years

Huge heart
Blue whales need a big heart to pump huge amounts of blood around their body. A blue whale heart weighs about the same as a MINI Cooper car—700 kilograms (1,540 lb).

10-year-old boy
1.4 m (4.5 ft)

Filter Feeder
Blue Whale

Male blue whale
25 m (82 ft)

Blue whales are the largest animals known to have lived on Earth. They are found throughout the world, but the biggest creatures live around Antarctica. The longest ever recorded was a massive 33.6 metres (110.2 ft). The heaviest was 190 tonnes (209 tons), more than 15 times the weight of a double-decker bus. These enormous animals feed on tiny marine creatures. They spend the summer at their feeding grounds in polar seas, eating up to 3.6 tonnes (4 tons) of krill a day. In the winter they migrate to warmer waters, where they mate and give birth. Blue whales were hunted almost to extinction. Hunting of blue whales was banned in 1967, but numbers have not recovered.

Big gulp
A blue whale takes a huge gulp of water. Its throat can expand up to four times wider than normal and hold half its body volume in water.

Tail fluke *This is as wide as the wings of a small aircraft. The whale beats its tail to swim through the water—at up to 48 kilometres per hour (30 mph) when alarmed.*

UNKNOWN

LOWER RISK

VULNERABLE

ENDANGERED

Baleen bristles *The edges of the baleen are frayed to form bristles. These act like a sieve that water can pass through but krill gets caught on.*

Baleen plates *The whale has no teeth. Instead, a row of 300–400 baleen plates hangs on either side of its mouth. These are flat plates of keratin, the same material that is in human fingernails.*

Feeding time *Blue whales feed where the krill are thickest, down around 100 metres (328 ft) during the day. They only feed at the surface at night.*

Pleated throat *A series of pleats runs lengthways down the throat. These stretch during feeding and the throat expands up to four times wider than normal to gulp water and food.*

Giant sieve

Blue whales are filter feeders, sieving their tiny prey out of the water. After finding a dense swarm of krill, a blue whale opens its enormous mouth to take a gulp of up to 90 tonnes (99 tons) of water and food. It then closes its mouth and forces the water out with its strong throat muscles. The baleen plates on its jaws capture the food, which the whale then scrapes off with its tongue.

Naked sea butterfly, or cliones

Bristleworm

Krill

Tiny food for a giant

Blue whales feed on tiny marine animals. Shrimp-like krill form the main part of their diet. Climate change and commercial fishing are reducing krill numbers, which threatens the whale's survival.

Polar Life

ARCTIC FACTS

The North Pole
Located within the Arctic Ocean, the North Pole is Earth's northernmost point. Each year, in March, an area of the Arctic Ocean one and a half times the size of Canada is covered by sea ice. Over summer, the area of sea ice shrinks by more than half.

Coldest: −70°C (−94°F)
Hottest: 2°C (36°F)

Tromsø, Norway
Average precipitation
Average temperature

Arctic climate
Temperatures in the Arctic do not fall as low as those in the Antarctic because the Arctic region centres about an ocean. The annual average temperature for the Arctic is 10°C (50°F). Tromsø is a city in the far north of Norway, 350 kilometres (217 mi) north of the Arctic Circle.

ANTARCTIC FACTS

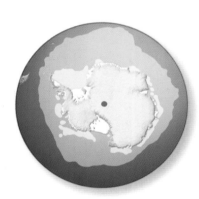

The South Pole
The southernmost point on Earth, the South Pole is located on land, within the continent of Antarctica. The amount of sea ice around Antarctica changes from season to season. The most sea ice is seen around September, whereas the smallest amount is in February.

Coldest: −89.2°C (−128.6°F)
Hottest: 15°C (59°F)

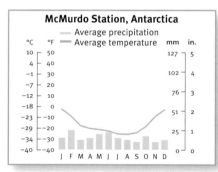

McMurdo Station, Antarctica
Average precipitation
Average temperature

Antarctic climate
Antarctica is the coldest, windiest continent on Earth. It is classified as desert because so little rain or snow falls there. McMurdo Station is an American research centre on the coast of Antarctica. The average temperature for the whole of Antarctica is −60°C (−79°F).

LAND OF THE MIDNIGHT SUN

Midnight Sun
During polar summers, the Sun doesn't set for weeks at a time, which has led to polar regions being called the "land of the midnight Sun". This time-lapse photograph, taken at regular intervals, shows the Sun moving towards the horizon in Norway but not going below it. Polar winters are very dark because the Sun does not rise above the horizon for weeks.

ANIMALS IN DANGER

The International Union for Conservation of Nature (IUCN) has developed a Red List of Threatened Species that indicates the conservation status of animal and plant species. Endangered species are those thought to have a very high risk of becoming extinct; vulnerable species have a high risk level.

ENDANGERED

Blue whale

VULNERABLE

Rockhopper penguin

Humpback whale

Polar bear

Grey-headed albatross

Northern fur seal

Macaroni penguin

Beluga

UNKNOWN

Colossal squid

LOWER RISK

Ringed seal

Willow ptarmigan

Orca

Musk ox

Bowhead whale

Leopard seal

Walrus

Adélie penguin

Arctic fox

Grey wolf

Atlantic puffin

Emperor penguin

Arctic stoat

PEOPLE

Scientific research
Equipment carried by weather balloons measures wind speed, wind direction, temperature and humidity. Large weather balloons can fly high enough to measure ozone levels in the upper atmosphere.

Fresh water
One thing that is not in short supply in the Arctic is fresh water. Simply melt the snow and you have some of the cleanest water in the world.

Precision sewing
In Barrow, Alaska, Inuit women sew seal skins together to make an "umiak", a type of boat. To keep water from seeping through the seams, it is essential to use tiny stitches that do not form holes in the furs being joined.

Glossary

AD An abbreviation for the Latin "anno Domini", meaning "in the year of our Lord". Used for the measurement of time, AD indicates the number of years since the supposed date of Christ's birth.

Antarctic The region around the South Pole.

Antarctic circle An imaginary line around Earth marking the edge of the Antarctic. Everywhere south of this line has at least one day a year when the Sun does not rise and one day a year when it does not set.

Arctic The region around the North Pole.

Arctic circle As for the Antarctic circle, but around the Arctic.

aurora Display of red, green and occasionally blue light in the sky. It is called the aurora borealis or northern lights in the Arctic, and the aurora australis or southern lights in the Antarctic.

baleen plates Plates with frayed edges made out of keratin, the same material as hair and fingernails. Found in the mouths of certain whales instead of teeth, they are used for filter feeding.

blubber Layer of fat found under the skin of a bird or mammal. Important as a layer of insulation.

calving The process by which icebergs break off glaciers or ice shelves.

camouflage The way an animal blends into its environment to sneak up on prey or avoid enemies.

canine teeth The teeth between the front incisors and the side molars of mammals.

carbon dioxide (CO2) A colourless, odourless gas formed when fuels and materials are burnt, and by living organisms as they live, die and rot.

carnivore An animal that eats meat.

cephalopod molluscs A group of invertebrates that includes octopus, cuttlefish and squid. Characterised by their large brains, the name cephalopod means "head foot".

climate The weather that occurs in a region over a long period of time. The climate in a desert area, for example, is hot and dry.

conservation Looking after Earth's resources for future generations.

crustacean A large group of invertebrates that includes shrimps, krill, crabs, lobsters, barnacles, woodlice and others. They have a hard outer skeleton with joints in the legs and along their bodies to allow movement.

cusp A pointed or rounded lump on the biting surface of a tooth.

dentine A hard material made largely from calcium phosphate minerals. It forms most of the tooth, and is usually covered in enamel.

dorsal fin The fin on the back of a fish or whale.

echolocation A system used by bats and certain whales and dolphins to detect objects in their environment. These animals listen for the echoes of their calls to locate prey or to aid navigation.

ecosystem Describes the animals, plants, climate and other factors that interact and function together in a particular area.

endangered species Animals likely to die out completely unless people take action to save them.

expedition A journey, often over a long distance, with a goal to reach a particular place, or discover new information.

extinct No longer living. When the last living member of a species dies, the species is extinct.

filter feeder An animal that eats very small prey by sieving it out of water.

fish A group of vertebrate animals adapted to living in water, with gills for breathing.

firn A layer near the top of a glacier or ice sheet that is half way between snow and glacial ice.

fledging The process by which young birds develop their adult feathers and leave the nest to fend for themselves.

fossil fuels Coal, oil and gas. These fuels are formed over millions of years from the remains of plants and animals.

frazil ice Small ice crystals that form on the ocean surface when it reaches freezing temperature.

frostbite A condition where the skin and other tissues freeze when exposed to extremely cold temperatures.

glacial ice Ice that has formed on land from compacted snow.

glacier A huge mass of ice formed from compacted snow, which slowly flows across land over thousands of years.

global warming An observed increase in the average temperature of Earth's atmosphere.

greenhouse effect The process by which gases in Earth's atmosphere trap solar radiation, absorbing it and bouncing it back to Earth to heat the atmosphere, oceans and surface.

greenhouse gases Gases, such as carbon dioxide and methane, in Earth's atmosphere that contribute to the greenhouse effect.

habitat The area in which a plant or animal lives.

herbivore An animal that eats plants.

hibernation A kind of "deep sleep" used by some animals over winter to reduce the amount of energy they use. A hibernating animal lowers its body temperature and slows its breathing and heart rates.

hypothermia A serious medical condition suffered when body temperature drops below the level needed to function normally.

ice breaker A ship designed to break through sea ice on the surface of the ocean.

ice floe A flat, free moving piece of sea ice, usually less than 10 kilometres (6 mi) long.

ice sheet A large mass of glacial ice on land. Ice sheets can be several kilometres thick and cover areas up to 50,000 square kilometres (20,000 sq mi).

ice shelf A large slab of glacial ice that floats on the water but is still attached to an ice sheet. The largest ice shelves in the world are in the Antarctic.

iceberg Large, floating pieces of glacial ice that have broken off glaciers or ice shelves.

incisors The teeth found at the front of the mouth in mammals.

incubation The process by which birds keep their eggs warm, usually by using their own body heat.

indigenous Native to a particular area.

insects A large group of small animals with three-part bodies, six legs and usually two pairs of wings. It includes flies, mosquitoes, bees and ants.

insulate To prevent heat from escaping.

Inuit A group of Arctic people who live in Canada, Alaska, Greenland and the north-east tip of Asia.

invertebrates Animals without backbones, including insects, squid, octopus, jellyfish, crabs, sponges and many others.

krill Tiny, shrimp-like animals found in the zooplankton that form a major part of the diet of animals such as the blue whale.

litter A group of newly born animals from the same mother at a single birth.

mammals A group of vertebrates that feeds its young with milk. It includes cats, dogs, whales, wolves, musk oxen, polar bears and people, among other creatures.

mate A partner during courtship and mating.

migration Seasonal movement of a group of animals from one place to another, often for breeding purpose or in search of food.

molars The side "cheek" teeth of a mammal.

moulting The process by which birds or mammals shed old, worn feathers or fur and replace them with new ones.

muscle Tissue made of elastic fibres, which pull and relax to make an animal move.

nautical mile A measure of distance. A nautical mile is equal to 1,852 metres (6,076.1 ft).

nest A pocket-like structure, often made of twigs, branches and grass. Many birds build nests in which to lay and incubate eggs, and to feed young.

nilas ice A smooth sheet of ice on the surface of the ocean when frazil ice crystals fuse together.

oesophagus Sometimes called the gullet or food pipe, this is the tube that takes food from the mouth down to the stomach.

organism Any living thing of any size.

ozone layer The thin layer of ozone gas, roughly 24 kilometres (15 mi) above Earth's surface that shields us from the Sun's ultraviolet rays.

pack ice Solid sea ice formed by wind and waves pushing smaller pieces of ice together.

palate The roof of the mouth.

pancake ice Irregular plates of ice formed when ice crystals fuse on the surface of a turbulent ocean.

permafrost Soil frozen for two or more years.

phytoplankton Tiny plants that form the basis of all ocean food chains.

plankton Tiny marine plants and animals.

plumage A bird's feathers.

pollution The contamination of air, water or land with harmful substances.

pores Tiny openings in skin or other structures.

predator An animal that hunts, kills and eats other animals (prey) to survive.

prey An animal that is hunted, killed and eaten by other animals (predators).

propulsion The process of driving or moving something in one direction.

range The entire geographic area across which a species is regularly found.

regurgitate To bring food back into the mouth from where it was stored in the stomach or crop.

Sami A group of Arctic people from northern Scandinavia.

scurvy A disease caused by a lack of vitamin C. It can cause skin and gum problems and lead to tooth loss.

sea ice Ice that forms when the surface of the ocean freezes.

snow blindness Loss of vision caused by bright sunlight reflected off pale surfaces of snow and ice.

species A group of animals with similar features. Members of a species can breed and have young.

streamlined Shaped to offer the least resistance to movement.

sub-Antarctic Describes places in the area just north of the Antarctic circle.

temperate Describes the zone extending from the tropics towards the poles, where winters and summers are mild, without extreme temperatures.

tundra A region characterized by low temperatures and populated with low-growing plants. The soil is usually frozen, and the amount of precipitation (rain and snow) is low.

tusks The long teeth of walruses, narwhals and elephants; used in fights, displays and defence.

ungulates Large, plant-eating mammals with hooves. They include musk oxen, goat, caribou, horses, deer, antelope and wild cattle.

vertebrates Animals with backbones, such as fish, amphibians, reptiles, birds and mammals.

warm-blooded Describes animals that maintain a constant, high body temperature by producing their own body heat. Mammals and birds are warm-blooded.

whiskers Sensitive hairs, usually quite stiff, found on the snout of certain mammals.

wingspan The straight distance from the tip of one wing to the tip of the other wing.

zooplankton Tiny animals that live in the ocean's surface layers.

Index

Credits

The publisher thanks Bronwyn Sweeney and Maria Harding for their contributions, and Jo Rudd for the index.

Key tl=top left, t=top, tc=top centre, tr=top right, cl=centre left, c=centre, cr=centre right, bl=bottom left, bc=bottom centre, bcr=bottom centre right, br=bottom right

MAPS
Andrew Davies/Creative Communication

ILLUSTRATIONS
Front cover Leonello Calvetti c, cr; Contact Jupiter/Polygone Studios br; **Back cover** Peter Bull Art Studios tr, c, bl; **Spine** Contact Jupiter/Yvan Meunier
Peter Bull Art Studio 8–9, 10–11, 18–19, 20–1, 22–3, 24–5, 26–7, 28–9, 30–1, 32–3, 38 t, tr, 40–1, 46–7, 52–3, 56 tr; **Leonello Calvetti** 8 cl, bl, 9 cr, 12–13, 36–7, 48–9, 54–5, 58–9; **Contact Jupiter/Yvan Meunier** 16–17, 44–5, 50–1; **Contact Jupiter/Polygone Studios** 14–15, 42–3; **Christer Eriksson** 38–9, 56–7

PHOTOGRAPHS
CBT=Corbis; GI=Getty Images; MP=Minden Pictures; NASA=National Aeronautics and Space Administration; NHPA=Natural History Photographic Agency; NPL=Nature Picture Library; SH=Shutterstock; SPL=Science Photo Library; TPL=photolibrary.com

10tr TPL, bl CBT; **13**bl TPL, bc TPL; **14**tr CBT; **15**cr1 MP, cr2 MP; **20**cl GI; **25**bc MP; **28**bc GI; **30**cl NASA, bl NASA; **32**bl SPL; **37**br SH; **38**cr CBT, bl CBT; **39**tc CBT; **42**bl MP; **43**tr MP; **54**cr NHPA; **58**bl NPL; **60**bcr CBT; **61**tr CBT, cr TPL, br CBT

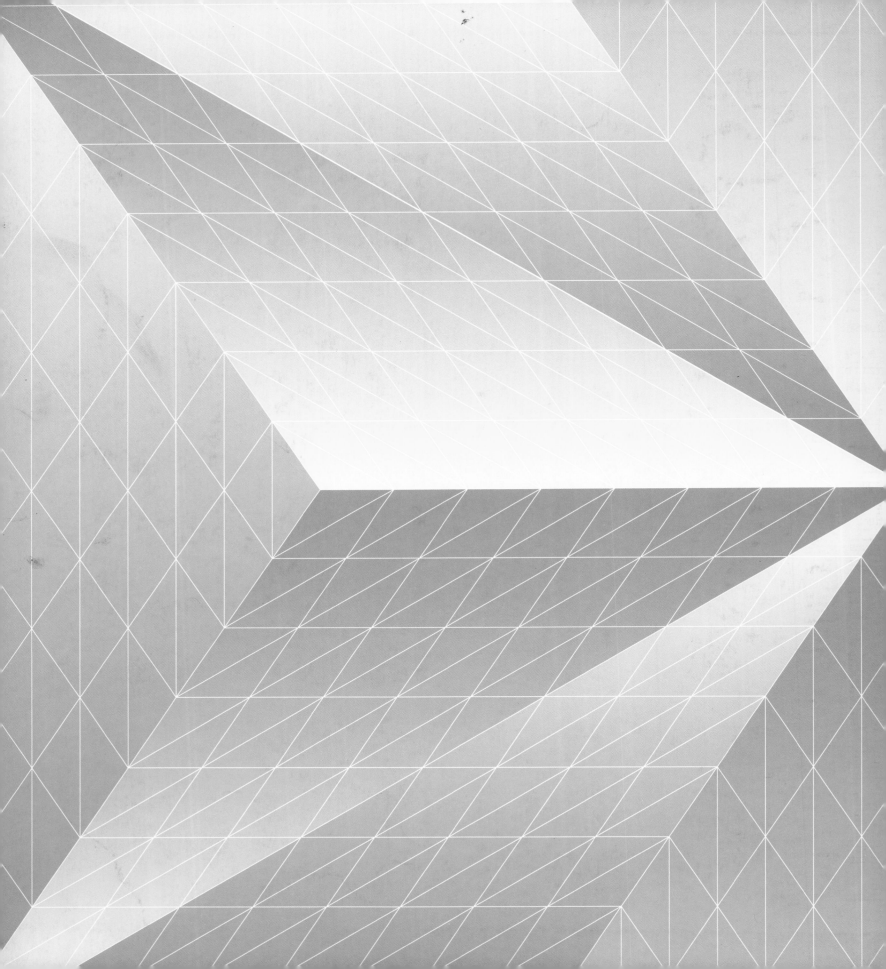